Meet Edgar Degas

National Gallery of Canada

Anne Newlands

J. B. LIPPINCOTT

NEW YORK

Meet Edgar Degas
Text copyright Education Services, National Gallery of Canada,
National Museums of Canada © 1988

First published by Kids Can Press Ltd., Toronto, Ontario, Canada

1   2   3   4   5   6   7   8   9   10

First American Edition, 1989

Library of Congress Cataloging-in-Publication Data
Degas, Edgar, 1834–1917.
    Meet Edgar Degas.

    Also issued in French under title: Voici Edgar Degas.
    Summary: Presents the life and paintings of Edgar
Degas in a first person narrative drawn from letters,
notebooks, and people's stories about the artist.
    1. Degas, Edgar, 1834–1917 —Juvenile literature.
2. Artists—France—Biography—Juvenile Literature.
[1. Degas, Edgar, 1834–1917.   2. Artists]   I. Newlands,
Anne.   II. National Gallery of Canada.   III. Title.
N6853.D33D38 1988   709'.2'4 [B] [92]   88-32035
ISBN 0-397-32369-7

Edgar Degas was luckier than many painters: he was famous during his long lifetime and his work was much in demand. Yet Degas was still a rebel. He feuded with other artists and battled with the art critics. Some were angered because his work was not pretty. Others were insulted because he thought they were fools.

Degas was born more than 150 years ago, before people knew how to record voices, so we don't know exactly what he sounded like. But we do know many things about his character, thanks to letters and notebooks he left behind and other peoples' stories about him. These tell us that he loved to talk and argue about art, politics and life.

In this book we have given Edgar Degas a voice that we hope suits him. We will talk with him in the busy streets and shops of Paris, in the theatres and at the racetrack, in the noisy cafés and in the quiet of his studio.

Let's meet Edgar Degas and look at his pictures with him.

Bonjour! I am Edgar Degas

If I seem to be staring at you, I'm not. I'm staring at myself, in a mirror. Try staring at yourself. In no time you'll start to squirm.

When you paint a self-portrait you stare hard at yourself. As you look at your face you try to figure out what is happening behind it, in your mind. There are so many questions: Do I like myself? Do other people like me? Am I talented? Am I handsome or funny-looking? Who am I?

When I painted this picture I was 23 years old. How serious I looked. I studied my features for hours—the way the light hit my face and the way my eyes stood out from the shadow cast by my hat.

One question—What was I going to be?—was easy. I boldly painted my answer. I made my orange scarf and white smock very bright, so people would notice them right away. "Aha!" they would say. "This fellow is an artist!"

Self-Portrait in a Soft
Hat *1857–58*
Oil on paper mounted on canvas
26 x 19 cm
10¼ x 7½ in
Sterling and Francine Clark Art Institute, Williamstown, Massachusetts

The Young Spartans

In my day painting was supposed to be dignified. (Humph!) Paintings, people said, should be about heroic subjects from history.

But I didn't want to draw heroes or conquerors or scenes from the past. I wanted to draw real, live people. I wanted to understand how they walk and stretch and sit and dance. But I also wanted to become known as an artist. So I decided to compromise: I'd do some of what other people wanted and some of what I wanted.

My young Spartans are ordinary people. The boys are exercising, each in a different position. One girl challenges the boys, but no one seems to take up her dare. The older people just chat in the background.

After I did a few more of these history pictures, I grew tired of painting people who lived thousands of years ago. So I made a very important decision: I would paint *my* world and the people in it.

Young Spartans
c. 1860–62
Oil on canvas
109 x 155 cm
42⅞ x 61 in
The Trustees of the
National Gallery,
London

My Italian Relatives

This picture may look like a simple portrait of a family, but more than that, it tells the story of their life together.

Laura Bellelli, the mother in the picture, is my favourite aunt. Do you think she looks sad? Her father—my grandfather—has died and she had just returned from his funeral when I began the first sketches for the painting. I have placed a drawing of my grandfather in the picture frame near Aunt Laura's head. My aunt and my cousins are in mourning: they will wear black clothing and will not go to dances or concerts or give parties for many months.

During sad times, people hope to be comforted by their families, but this does not always happen. Aunt Laura's marriage to the Baron Bellelli is not a very happy one. He sits with his back to us as if he doesn't want to be in the picture at all. But at least my aunt has her daughters close to her, and they seem strong together.

As you can see, my two cousins are very different. Giovanna looks out at us, her hands quietly folded in front of her. But as hard as she tries, Giulia cannot sit still. She twists impatiently in her chair. I think both she and the dog would like to get away.

This is one of my largest paintings—two metres (more than six feet) high. I couldn't work on such a large painting in my aunt's apartment. So I made separate sketches of each family member and did the painting later in Paris. Here is my sketch of Giulia, daydreaming. Is she looking a little sad—or maybe a little bored?

The Bellelli Family
1858–67
Oil on canvas
200 x 250 cm
78¾ x 98⅜ in
Musée d'Orsay, Paris

Giulia Bellelli *(study for*
The Bellelli Family)
Essence on paper
mounted on panel
38.5 x 26.7 cm
15⅛ x 10½ in
Dumbarton Oaks
Research Library and
Collection, Washington

My Musical Friends

My friend Désiré Dihau is usually placed near the back of the orchestra, so that the lovely sounds from his bassoon don't drown out the violins. But I have put him and some other friends front and centre. They don't play together in real life. And some of them aren't musicians at all. But my orchestra is for the eyes, not the ears!

A seat close to the orchestra is reserved especially for you. In front of you are the musicians and, above them, a thin slice of the stage. You can see a blur of legs and costumes behind the black curved neck of the double bass. My friends in their black suits look very serious as they make music for the pink and blue fantasy on stage.

My picture has captured the brief moment when you take your eyes from the dancers and look straight ahead. I wanted to show you how people really see the world—just a glimpse at a time.

The Orchestra of the
Opéra, *c. 1870*
Oil on canvas
56.5 x 46.2 cm
22¼ x 18¼ in
Musée d'Orsay, Paris

Practice Makes Perfect

A critic once said that if you saw my ballet paintings, you didn't have to go to a live performance. It was meant as a compliment, so I didn't want to tell him that he had missed the point. I am fascinated not so much by the dance as by the way the human body moves. For me, the ballet is a good place to study motion.

We are watching a class at the Paris Opéra. Light shines through the large windows outside the picture frame. The dancers look delicate in their crisp, white dresses, but they are really as strong as horses. Their grace comes from hard work, sweat and pain. The ballerinas around the walls are stretching their legs and feet so their muscles will not stiffen up. But everyone else is still. The dancer in the middle of the room is poised to begin. The violinist waits for the signal to play. At a word from the ballet master in the white suit, the room will come alive.

Dance Class at the Opéra
1872
Oil on canvas
32 x 46 cm
12⅝ x 18⅛ in
Musée d'Orsay, Paris

What a Star!

We are watching the ballet from a box seat at the side of the theatre. From here we can look down at the dancer and also see what's happening beside the stage, in the "wings."

The star is alone on the huge dark stage. She shimmers in the bright light, her outstretched arms forming an elegant curve. She seems to balance effortlessly on one leg. But look closely. Could this leg really support her? Perhaps not, but that didn't matter to me as much as showing how light and shadow can make a figure seem to move.

The other dancers are offstage, waiting behind the scenery and watching the magic of the dance. A man dressed in black—perhaps a friend of the star—also watches from the wings.

The Star, *1876–77*
Pastel over monotype
58 x 42 cm
22¹³/₁₆ x 16½ in
Musée d'Orsay, Paris

The Fourteen-year-old Dancer

This is Marie van Goethem, a 14-year-old dance student at the Paris Opéra. She is not unusual—neither pretty nor very talented. But because I chose her as a model for my sculpture, she is now famous.

I made my sculpture out of wax, which I tinted a flesh colour. I bought a wig at a puppet store and tied it up with a ribbon. I dressed her in a real ballet costume and silk slippers and covered everything but the skirt with wax. And there she stands, holding her head proudly!

When my sculpture was first exhibited, people were uncomfortable looking at her. But they couldn't tear themselves away. They were fascinated because she looked so lifelike, all dressed and almost two-thirds her natural size. They expected to see a beautiful ballet dancer. But Marie is just herself—skinny, small and homely.

My sculpture caused an uproar! People were furious, and I was delighted!

The Little Fourteen-Year-Old Dancer *c. 1881*
Wax, silk, satin ribbon, hair
height 99 cm
39 in
Mr. and Mrs. Paul Mellon, Upperville, Virginia

A Moving Picture

You may think this is a group of dancers before they go on stage, but look more closely, for I am very cunning. It is not a group—I made this picture up from sketches and drawings of one dancer in several poses. I created a setting for the poses by adding stage scenery, extra figures in the background and the silhouette of a man.

When I put the sketches together, my dancer appears to move. First she faces us: her head is down and her hands are on her hips. Then she turns her back to us and leans into the stage set. As she walks around it she raises her head and moves her arms, first to her shoulder and then higher, to fix her hair. At any moment, she could step on stage and dance.

Dancers, Pink and Green
c. 1890
Oil on canvas
82.2 x 75.6 cm
32³⁄₈ x 29³⁄₄ in
The Metropolitan Museum of Art, New York
Bequest of Mrs. H.O. Havemeyer 1929. The H.O. Havemeyer Collection

A Man of His Times

Henri Rouart is an engineer and a manufacturer, so I painted him in front of the factory he owns. I have linked him to the factory by the lines of railway track, but I made Henri bigger and more important.

Why did I paint Henri at his work? Why not in his home, surrounded by rich furniture and beautiful objects? Because his factory is splendid, and he is proud of it. And because it shows him as a man of his times—as an industrialist.

Rouart is a very scientific fellow. He loves to solve practical problems, and he is very inventive. So I have focused my picture the way a camera, a recent invention, would. Henri's strong face and head are close up so they are very sharp. The building is in the distance so it is not as clear.

But even a painting with a factory in it doesn't tell everything. Henri Rouart and I were schoolmates and in the army together. He is also a painter and art collector. Most important, he is my very best friend.

Henri Rouart in Front of His Factory, *c. 1875*
Oil on canvas
65.1 x 50.2 cm
25⅝ x 19¾ in
The Carnegie Museum of Art, Pittsburgh
(Acquired through the generosity of the Sarah Mellon Scaife Family)

Off to the Races

I love going to the racetrack! Luckily, there is one quite close to my house, right in the city.

The upper picture shows what you would see there. I have even included the factory smokestacks in the distance. It is just a couple of minutes before the race begins. The horses are warming up, going every which way on the track. Some are calm, some jumpy. Occasionally one gets a bit skittish and has to be brought under control by the jockey. We see the track before us and the grandstand in the distance, as if we are on horseback with the jockeys.

I drew the lower picture 25 years later. You'll notice quite a difference. This picture is more like a dream: faceless jockeys ride horses going in all directions, creating a blur of movement.

For most people, the racetrack and the ballet were good entertainment. But for me, they were places to study figures in motion. And that's why I came back to these subjects again and again, always finding new ways of painting them.

Racehorses Before the Stands, *c. 1866–68*
Essence on paper
mounted on canvas
46 x 61 cm
18⅛ x 24 in
Musée d'Orsay, Paris

Racehorses *1895–1900*
Pastel on paper
54 x 63 cm
21¼ x 24¾ in
National Gallery of
Canada, Ottawa

Dog Song

It's a lovely summer evening and we are going to one of my favourite places, the Alcazar d'Été, to listen to a singer. The customers at this café-concert are rowdy and cheerful, so a singer has to have a good set of lungs to be heard above the noise.

Thérésa has a wonderful voice, and she never has difficulty holding my attention. Here she is singing and acting out a song about a dog. See how she holds up her "paws." Do you think her plump face looks a bit like a dog's muzzle? She is doing an excellent imitation, and I admire her very much.

Tonight the audience is restless. People come and go beneath the gaslights and shadowy trees. But our eyes stay fixed on Thérésa, who shines against the darkness.

The Song of the Dog
c. 1876–77
Gouache and pastel over monotype
57.5 x 45.4 cm (image)
22⅝ x 17⅛ in
Private collection

A New Hat

In my day, many people wore different clothing for mornings, for afternoons, for doing errands and for paying visits. There was clothing for parties and clothing for the opera, clothing for the city and clothing for the country. Well-dressed women and men changed their clothes—and their hats—several times a day. Everyone wore a hat when going out.

This woman has come to the milliner's shop to buy herself a new hat. Have you ever watched people look at themselves in the mirror? Some stand very straight. Some scowl at their reflection. Others make funny faces. Let's sit and watch the woman stare at herself. The shop assistant is probably watching too, but I have hidden her behind the mirror. All our attention is on the customer. Do you think she will buy that hat?

If you could only shift in your chair, you might be able to see what the shop assistant looks like. Imagine how different the picture would be then.

At the Milliner's
1882
Pastel on paper
75.6 x 85.7 cm
29¾ x 33¾ in
The Metropolitan Museum of Art, New York
Bequest of Mrs. H.O. Havemeyer, 1929. The H.O. Havemeyer Collection

The Ironers

For these women ironing is hot, tiring work. All day every day they wash and iron other people's clothes. If they scorch the material they might lose their job. They keep a bottle of water handy to dampen the clothes.

The women are at work in a small, stuffy room. First they heat the flat-bottomed irons on the stove. Then they lift the irons from the stove to the table, where they press them down hard on the dampened laundry. When the irons cool they put them back on the stove. Then they start all over again. Lift, carry, bend, stretch. Lift, carry, bend, stretch. No wonder one of them is yawning.

Not all workers are as attractive as dancers, jockeys and singers. But the slow, steady movements of these large, plain women seen in the soft, warm light have a beauty all their own.

Women Ironing
c. 1884–86
Oil on canvas
76 x 81 cm
29¹⁵/₁₆ x 31⅞ in
Musée d'Orsay, Paris

The Bather

Oh yes, I too have seen all those graceful pictures and sculptures of ancient goddesses washing themselves. "How beautiful!" people say. "How noble!" But paint a real person quietly taking an ordinary bath and they are shocked. "Why waste your talents on such things?" they ask.

A waste? Not for me! I have spent my whole life carefully planning pictures to look as if I have merely captured a casual moment of daily life.

Take this picture, for example. A woman is having her back washed. She sits on the edge of the tub, stretching and leaning forward and supporting her weight on her left arm. With her right hand, she holds her hair up so it won't get wet when the water is poured down her back. We don't see her face. It is her pose that has caught my eye. It creates interesting shapes, shadows and colours for my painting.

Woman at Her Bath
c. 1895
Oil on canvas
71 x 89 cm
28 x 35⅜ in
The Art Gallery of
Ontario, Toronto

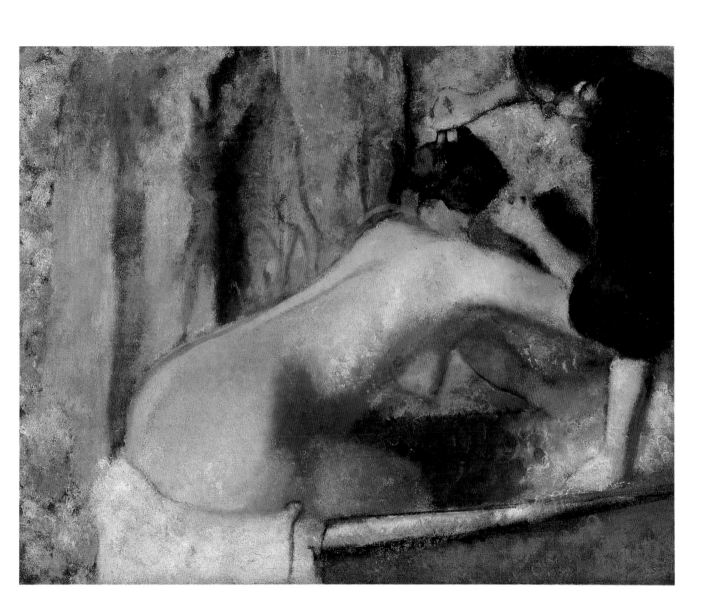

Edgar Degas lived a long life, 83 years in all. During that time the world changed enormously. Scientists found new ways of exploring the universe. Inventions such as the camera and the automobile changed the way people saw themselves and lived.

During his last years, Degas's sight and hearing weakened and he became locked inside his thoughts. His beloved house in the Rue Victor Massé was demolished to make way for new buildings. It was as if the world no longer had a place for him.

Degas died in 1917, but his art has kept alive the dancers, jockeys, ironers, café singers and musicians who lived in Paris a century ago. Today his paintings, drawings and sculptures remain for us to enjoy.

Hilaire Germain Edgar Degas
1834 – 1917